# WHEN
# YOU ARE A
# SINGLE PARENT

"Romance fails us and so do friendships, but the relationship of parent and child, less noisy than all others, remains indelible and indestructable, the strongest relationship on earth."

Theodor Reik, *Of Love and Lust*

# WHEN
# YOU ARE A
# SINGLE PARENT

*Robert C. DiGiulio*

# ABBEY PRESS
St. Meinrad, Indiana 47577

To my wonderful parents: Angela and the late
    Thomas DiGiulio, Sr.

To Christine Jean, Christine Ann, Aimee, and Katie
    Ann DiGiulio.

To T.O.P.

PHOTOS: Deborah Churan, Cover; Randy Dieter, page 8; Jean-Claude Lejeune, pages 18 and 40; Greg Roberts, page 28; Kay Freeman, pages 49 and 88; Strix Pix, pages 58 and 69; Charles Quinlan, page 84, Bob Smith, page 92.

Library of Congress Catalog Card Number:
79-53274
ISBN: 0-87029-154-8

# CONTENTS

# Foreword

## A Responsibility, a Challenge, and an Opportunity

Lonely? Yes. If you are a single parent, the days following separation from your spouse can be a time of absolute desolation. But *alone*? Not necessarily. Because you are a single parent, your life—now—with your children takes on even more importance than in the past. There is no denying that it will seem more difficult at times, for, if being a parent is a great responsibility (and it is), being a single parent seems like an even greater responsibility.

But with that responsibility comes a *challenge* to make your life with your child something special. Certainly, your life—and your child's life—has changed radically. But, whether you are divorced or widowed, this is the truly wonderful part: you're still alive; you're still a parent. Whether you have custody, or your former spouse has custody, you are still *you*. And, to your child, that "you" can mean the world. Not only can you continue to have a positive effect on your child's life, but you can take the opportunity to magnify it as well.

Children have little power to influence the kind of childhood they will have. A child has absolutely no ability to influence the kind of parent he or she is born to. Thus, only you—as parent—have that unique *opportunity* to make your child's life with you something special: a close and loving relationship—even if such did not exist in the past. It is an opportunity to start again, to make some changes in the way you choose to share your life with your child. Don't look at it as "the long road back," or "putting the pieces together," because nothing between you and your child was broken; nothing between you need be repaired. Whether you are a mother or a father, you still have your very precious and wonderful relationship with your child, and you have the opportunity to make that relationship even better than it might have been in the past.

You have the power to choose. You can choose to be the kind of parent that can help your child live a full, healthy, and happy life. No one else can do it—except you.

# CHAPTER 1
# Single through Death

I know what bereavement means. When I was a teenager, my father died. Although he was sick for a few years preceding his death and did not die suddenly, nothing could have been more unexpected to my adolescent mind. He was forty-seven years old. And so was my mother. Maybe I can shed some light on the problem of being a widowed parent . . . from the point of view of a child.

After he died, I went to sleep each night crying into my pillow, "Why did you have to leave me, Dad? Why?" My first feelings of grief were very personal. I had few thoughts—those first few days—about my mother, my brother, or my sister. To simply talk to them about Dad was unbearable, since all it would lead to would be more tears, more sadness.

I felt numb. Nothing could have prepared me for that experience. I couldn't accept his death (and in a way, I still haven't), because I still felt his presence. I "got used to" his not being there, because "accepting" his death seemed at least a superhuman act.

Eventually, after a few weeks, I found myself getting caught up again in school routines. My little sister was with her friends again, and my brother was a newlywed setting up his home with his wife. It was now just the three of us: Mom, my sister Ann, and I. Soon I came to realize that my life was going forward rather normally, but I also realized — almost suddenly — that my mother's days *were not*. When I left for school in the morning, she was sitting at the kitchen table; when I came home at 3:30 PM, she was still sitting at that same spot at the kitchen table. She was there — just *there*. And that's when something happened: I began to kiss her each morning when I left and each afternoon when I came home. Although I had done that regularly as a very young child, I had gradually stopped when I was in the sixth grade, because I was (or so I thought) "too old for that sort of stuff."

What became very clear to me from my deepest unconscious mind was this understanding: *Someday, this wonderful person will not be with me any longer just as my Dad is no longer here. Let me let her know that I love her — now — because we don't know about tomorrow or next week. She's here right now, and so am I, so let me be with her as much as I can.* As much as I missed my dad, there was nothing I could do to bring him back, or to bring a smile to his face one more time, or to show my love for him. *Except one thing.* There was something I could do: love and assist that person he loved so deeply, Mom. Although my sister and I didn't plan how we would respond, we both understood and sensed that Mom was pretty shaken, and that she needed us very much at this time in her life.

But what could we do to help make Mom happy again? How could we help this normally joyful person do more than show just an occasional tearful smile? How could two kids ever replace Dad?

Within a short few months, the answer became apparent. Get her out of the kitchen, out of the house! She needed *more* than her children, her laundry, and her worries. After twenty-five years of being a mother, homemaker, and wife, she needed to learn how to start living again—to start living for herself and not just for us or for the house. Surely, our relatives were most supportive during our family crisis and were more than willing to help out with just about any request. We visited them frequently.

But there was another side to the coin. My sister and I realized that my mother's closest relatives, her sisters and brothers, were really constant reminders to Mom of her past life with our father. In short, each time we visited with them, they unintentionally helped Mom live in the past, helped her relive the days with her husband. This had to change. We wanted her to remember our beloved Dad, but at her young age, we wanted her to live for the *now* and for the future. We began to take action.

Our first step was to take Mom out to an excellent Italian restaurant—probably the first meal she had not cooked herself since my father became sick nine years before. Then came the most crucial part (a part that made all the difference), meeting some new *friends*. Mom at age forty-seven was a young widow. All her friends and relatives were married and totally immersed in their families. She needed new friends, and, through one of my friends at school, Mom met a single mother who was, like herself, recently widowed. Not having to face her widowhood alone, Mom soon began going out (at first it took a lot of coaxing on our parts) to movies, plays, shopping, and, eventually, dancing. All she really needed was a friend. A friend who could assure her that enjoying her life again wasn't wrong. And the spin-off effect was remarkable: within a relatively short period of time, she had established a new set of friends who shared her single parent state, but were *doers* instead of *mourners*. No black dresses for Mom! Eventually, Mom did remarry, and we welcomed Tom into our family. We will never forget Dad; we never could. But we couldn't forget Mom, either.

## A Growth Process

If bereavement is to have any meaning at all, it needs to be a growth process, a positive growth process. Which means that, after the bereavement (or as a result of it), a human being must be ready to live again. If all bereavement does is cause our spirits to die with the deceased, then it has served no positive purpose. Despite what some authors and experts say, I don't think we can ever really accept the death of a loved one. Certainly, we "get used to" the void and we go on living, but we find that our lives have changed. What is all important is whether we permit our lives to be changed for the better, or allow ourselves to give in, to quit. Every single parent who has lost his or her spouse through death needs to live, to look forward to something. And, all of those single parents who are living a happy life have *made* their lives happy. None has been "lucky"; not one has simply "been fortunate." What do they have in common? A desire to live that is even stronger now that they have seen death. They are people who have grieved long and hard, but they have drawn a line on that grieving and have begun living again.

No matter how hard it seems, you—as a single parent—still have that wonderful, precious, and often-difficult obligation called children, and that wonderful, precious, and even at times more-difficult obligation called *yourself*. As a child of a single parent, I grew up. I realized how precious my family was, because, quite bluntly, I understood that they would not be around—on earth, at least—forever. I had to live with them now, for them today, and in love with them forever.

With this understanding came the change in behavior. Just as I was no longer afraid of being "mushy" or "corny" when I kissed my Mom good-bye as I left for school, my sister, mother, and I did not think twice about showing our love in various ways. For example, we didn't care what our friends thought ("You drive your mother to the supermarket? What a drag!"), nor did we care about some of our relatives' reactions when my mother began seeing men ("How horrid! And he's only been dead two years!"). We were fortunate because we focused on ourselves. And we had (and still have) each other. We refused to accept guilt or allow misgivings to creep in, despite the best attempts of well-meaning friends and relatives. It was the most powerful time in our lives.

## Practical Suggestions

• **Include Your Child in Your Mourning.** If your family life is to go on, your child must share that important experience. We parents sometimes want to shelter our children from unpleasant experiences, and death has to be just about the most wrenching. You can not force or expect a child to accept death. It is something he or she will have to contend with as part of life, and, ultimately, learn to deal with personally. If the family can come around to re-establishing itself, then it has not been a death of the family. To shelter a child from the reality of the death itself can be a real injustice.

When you can handle it personally, speak openly and freely about your beloved spouse. Speak with your children and — always — let them speak to you about him or her. Try very hard (no matter how difficult it may seem at first) to avoid making "taboos" between yourself and your child. For example, there will be times when you do not want to be reminded of an incident or a story concerning the deceased, but, if your child really feels it is important enough to bring up, face it honestly and try to understand the need that is there.

• **Share with Relatives.** Just as the saying goes: "They were the best of times; they were the worst of times," when there is a death in the family, our relatives can be "the best of friends, the worst of friends." Ironically, they almost always mean well. Practically speaking, you need to draw the line on how much "help" you wish to receive from well-meaning relatives. Certainly, the love they feel for your former spouse cannot be denied, but don't let their caring for you and your child turn into a dictatorship. You are an adult, and you are perfectly competent to get your life together. You can handle the change in your life. Accept the help relatives can give, but avoid turning over to them "the reins of power" by allowing them to discipline your children, or by allowing them to try to act in place of your former spouse. "It's what he would have done if he were here" and "She would have wanted it this way" are popular lines used by others to get you to resist

14

changing your life for the better. Seek no one to do "what he or she would do," but instead, take control of the situation yourself. If you can accept help, without permitting it to become interference, you've taken a first step toward rebuilding your life with your children.

• **Renew Interests.** Regardless of the age of your children, you must get your own life back in shape after the bereavement. Naturally, the age of your children will influence your activity at first, but this should not prevent you from renewing old interests and even cultivating new ones.

• **Go Out.** Avoid, if at all possible, sedentary and placid activities. At least for now, read less, put your sewing kit or coin collection aside, and go out. There is a strong relationship between mind and body, so think about the effect of a tennis match with a good friend. Or, bowling, gymnastics, or slimnastics. Move around. Get that "tired-happy" feeling! Take up something new like dancing or relearn the backstroke at a neighborhood pool.

• **Be with People.** Be with happy people, and avoid morbid, depressing, and low-key personalities as much as possible. Don't try to be a "rock of Gibraltar" silently bearing your sadness. It does no one—least of all you—any good at all!

• **Make a Commitment.** Sometimes we *plan* to do glorious, exciting things, but somehow they never materialize. Why? No commitment was made! Here's one way to do it. Sign up for a course at a local high school, community college, or YMCA. Pay the fee, too, because that will be a strong incentive for you to go through with it. If you register for the bowling league, don't be the "alternate" who plays only if someone is absent.

• **Don't Volunteer.** Many people will recommend volunteering your time at schools or hospitals, but it is best not to do so too soon after the death of your spouse. You should—at first—think of nobody but yourself and your children. I know this might sound selfish, but the very nature of a volunteer's work makes him or her expendable, a "luxury" to the school or hospital. Come to feel good again about your own life first, then consider volunteer work. Naturally, there is nothing purer in terms of loving others than giving of yourself to help them. But unless you have regained yourself, you will have nothing to give.

• **Get a Sitter.** Even if you have young children, you are decidedly not a prisoner at home—to be at their disposal every waking (and sleeping) moment. You love your children, and you want to be a suitable parent for them. If you allow yourself time for your own interests, you will be a fuller, happier, and more positive parent for them.

• **Make New Friends.** If recently widowed, it is likely your circle of friends is limited to married couples. By all means, you want to keep them as friends, but try to involve yourself in situations where you can meet new people (such as bowling, swimming, dancing). It is amazing how effective "new blood" can be. By meeting new people, your whole outlook can change for the better. You've "accepted" the death of your spouse (at least as much as any human can ever "accept" death), and you are not alone in your predicament. Make yourself happy; meet your own needs. Because by doing so, you'll be able to be that much more of a parent and person to your children. New friends accept you for what you are *today*, right now; they won't tend to try to reshape you into what you were. If they are true friends, they won't attempt to impose their ideas of what you "should be." We all change as we go through life, and the death of a husband or wife can change you greatly. Accept the change, and surround yourself with those who accept and enjoy being with you.

# CHAPTER 2
# Single through Law

Jean is a single parent. She and Ben were married when they were both twenty, and, after ten stormy years of marriage, Jean filed for and received a divorce from Ben. That was eight years ago. Custody of their daughter Karen has been assigned to Jean since the divorce, and Ben has visited Karen, more or less regularly over the past eight years.

One of the factors involved in the parting of Jean and Ben was Ben's alcoholism and his often violent behavior when intoxicated. Jean was "guilty," too, of trying to hide his problems (*their* problems) from friends and in-laws. When Karen was five years old, Jean felt the time had come to make the decision to separate.

In the eight years since the divorce, Ben at first wavered between going on drinking binges and abstaining completely. He has not had a drink now in two years. When she left Ben, Jean took a small apartment near her parents, who took care of Karen during the day while Jean worked. After the divorce, Jean was faced with a new problem, her parents. They knew of Ben's alcoholic bouts, and they vehemently opposed the visitation agreement which allowed Ben to be with Karen on Sundays. Jean not only loved her parents, but needed them to watch her five-year-old Karen. Jean did not share her parents' deep hostility toward Ben, but simply made it clear to him that he could see Karen only if he was not intoxicated, and would not drink while he was with her. Ben agreed, but they couldn't convince her parents. Eventually, after one difficult year living near her parents, Jean moved, enrolled Karen in the first grade, and rented an apartment away from her parents.

When asked how she felt toward Ben and the visitation rights, Jean said: "As long as Ben understood how I felt toward his drinking, I didn't want to stand in the way of his seeing Karen. I never want Karen to accuse me of not letting her be with her father."

Jean can be taken as a model parent for at least one good reason: Her love for Karen was *unselfish*. Although Jean felt no real love or closeness toward Ben, she never allowed her personal feelings to stand in the way of the father-daughter relationship. She was wise, for Karen's well-being, to state limits, but Jean never belittled her former husband either to Karen or to others. Likewise, she avoided comparisons between her ability as a parent and Ben's. In short, she did not allow an otherwise "socially disgraceful" illness (alcoholism) to stand between Ben and Karen.

In fact, this true story (the names were changed) has a "happy ending," because Ben, Jean, and Karen have found their own lives fuller, and Karen now a teenager knows that, although her parents could not live together, they love her deeply — both of them.

In some ways, the case of Ben, Jean, and Karen might seem at first a bit unusual. But there was really only one element that made all the difference in the world as far as the well-being of Karen was concerned, i.e. *cooperation* between Ben and Jean. If I called Jean a "model parent," I'd have to include Ben, too. In spite of the fact that they were unable to continue living together, both adults still had that one person in common (Karen), and, in the face of all the difficulties presented by Ben's alcohol problems and Jean's parents, Karen has been able to grow up benefitting from that cooperation.

What was really at the heart of this little story? What was the basis for Jean's decision? How did Jean decide what to do when different conflicts presented themselves? As Jean explained: "I tried—all the time—to consider the best thing to do for Karen. Many times it would be like choosing between the 'frying pan and the fire,' but when I looked at it from my daughter's point of view, the choices were actually easy."

For example, Jean was undecided whether or not Karen should see her father at all in light of his problems with alcohol. If she did allow her daughter to be with him, there was the possibility that, indirectly, Karen would be harmed by his behavior. If she did not let Karen go with him, there was the real possibility that Karen would be missing her father's love and would deeply resent that. Another major "frying pan or fire" situation was living near her parents. If she stayed there, Karen would be watched by her grandparents, but would probably get—along with their love—a strong dose of hatred directed at her dad. By asserting her independence and moving away from her parents, Jean spared her daughter the tirades of her parents against Ben, although Grandma and Grandpa were welcome at Jean's new apartment.

In effect, Jean was a model of clear thinking for most divorced parents. When confronted with a single parent dilemma, you might profit if you ask yourself these two vital questions: "What's best for my child?" and "How can I make it possible?"

## Visitation Belongs to the Child

In a real sense, Jean and Ben were saying that visitation rights belonged not to either parent, but to their child. If visitation is a case of "your weekend" or "my weekend," the focus is away from the child, and you begin talking about a piece of property instead of a young human being. At the heart of this whole situation called "visitation" is *cooperation*. For the good of the child, both parents need to cooperate in all matters concerning the child. Why? Because, practically speaking, there are still two parents to the child. And, except in cases where mental illness or physical abuse is involved, both parents need to be real forces in the child's life.

Sometimes, the question, "Who will influence my child?" becomes a major concern of divorced parents. Occasionally, there is a feeling that the other parent is interfering. The tendency is natural for a parent to want to start over again after a divorce, and often this means a desire to exclude the noncustodial or less-present parent. The fact that there still are *two* parents cannot be forgotten, by either parent. With that in mind, how can parents achieve the relative harmony so dearly needed for the child's sake?

• **Accept the Custodial Parent.** Many divorced men and women have varying degrees of resentment and even anger toward their former spouses, especially, it seems, when their former spouses are the custodial parents. If this is the case with you, try very hard to remember that *your* importance to your child need not be diminished in any way simply because your former spouse has custody. Recognize that the word "custody" means just that: your child's day-to-day needs are being supervised by the custodial parent. That's all. It does not mean that your child will get "only her (or his) point of view," and that you are no longer important.

If you are the custodial parent, seek to work out matters concerning your child with your former spouse. It will make life better for that little person you both happen to love.

Ask yourself, "Am I taking out my anger *through* my child?" If so, no one will win. Deal openly with your angry or resentful feelings. Avoid using your child as a "sounding board," or requiring him or her to be a "little adult." Your child is a child; he or she cannot be expected to fully understand "your side of the story" and should be spared all conflict between you and your former spouse.

• **Look toward the Future.** Reliving the past with your child can only bring forth in him or her great resentment toward you and your former spouse. Your child is powerless to do anything about the established fact of your divorce, so living in the past or glorifying it serves no useful purpose. Instead, give yourself and your child something to look forward to, and not matters to regret.

• **Avoid Criticizing the Other Parent.** Most of the divorced men and women I know do complain about the way their former partner is bringing up the child. It seems that, after a divorce, the temptation to criticize the other is especially strong: "You're a lousy parent!" Criticism flows easily toward your estranged partner, especially when you're hurt. But, in serving your own wounded ego, you also serve to give your child a reason to be hurt, a reason to rebel and become bitter toward the other parent and to include you in this bitterness. To malign or put down your former spouse's competency as a parent, simply because your marriage didn't work out, might just boomerang on you. Even if you are not pleased with custodial or financial arrangements, try to adopt the attitude: "Speak well or not at all." For the sake of your child, accept your former spouse's shortcomings as a parent. He or she is trying, too!

• **Put Your Divorce in Perspective.** Especially if your child is old enough to request information about it. The very best way to handle it is to treat it in a matter-of-fact fashion. It won't be easy, because so much feeling is involved. But remember that your child cannot possibly grasp the degree of feeling, adult pride, or adult emotion that went into the never-pleasant event called "divorce." Therefore, avoid trying to convey those feelings to your child. They will just come across as a bewildering fabric of hurt. Try for the happy medium instead: "It wasn't a horrid personal failure. Nor was it "the best way." *The less emotional you can be* (and it will be difficult to avoid emotion!), *the more serenely your child will accept the fact of your divorce.*

Ironically, divorce can bring a new closeness between you and your child. Or, it can give you an excuse to get further away. By focusing your limited time on your child and by making those times happy, positive, and loving moments, you can still achieve your highest aspiration as a parent.

## Divorce and Insecurity

Divorce can increase a child's sense of insecurity. All children are, by nature of their age, insecure people. They need almost constant reassurance, and to us adults, it can seem like endless, annoying repetition. But just as surely as children need food and shelter, they need reassurance of their desirability (and lovability) as people. They might feel rejected, regardless of the real circumstances of the divorce. As always, a sincere smile, a hug, and a warm cuddle work much better than, "Yes, I love you. Stop asking me!"

All children have a normal degree of selfishness. This is related to their insecurity. Another way to look at "selfishness" is to see it as a simple statement of self-preservation. When we adults seek self-preservation, we are called "good workers" or "family minded." When children seek it, they are called "selfish."

The normal question in the back of any child's mind, as the parents go through the divorce process, is: "What does this divorce mean as far as *my life* is concerned? How will it affect me?" To face these questions squarely is the only way. Assure the child, through words and actions, that although life will be somewhat different now, your love and support will still be there. Place the emphasis on the child, rather than the "If-you-feel-bad-just-think-how-bad-I-feel" kind of statement.

Despite our best efforts, children often feel unloved or not worth loving after a divorce.

From one point of view, this is normal. All children, including you and I, feel—or felt—unloved as children at one time or another. But when there has been a divorce, those "unloved" feelings can take on mammoth proportions, especially when the parent feels somewhat guilty in the first place. You cannot avoid the issue, and trying to convince your child that he or she is indeed loved is probably a waste of

25

breath. Sure, words help, but there seems to be only one way to permanently counteract that "unloved" feeling in your children: live your love for your child; show it by your actions and not just your words. But it is often so hard to show love toward our children when we must work, tend to the house, and take care of a thousand other things. Certainly, one of the basic elements of loving is *time* — that most precious commodity to us adults. We never seem to have enough. There are three aspects of using the time you have toward banishing your child's "unloved," "What-will-become-of-me?" feelings. Without sacrificing the time needed for your normal adult activities, try *involvement, example,* and *attention*.

By *involvement* I mean having your child help wash dishes, set the table, or help as you change the oil in your car. Involvement lets a child say, "Hey, I count! I'm important!" Involvement means not simply saying that your child is important, but actually letting your child be important. After all, what's more precious and desirable than being important, useful, and helpful to Mom or to Dad?

Your *example* is simply how you act toward others, children and adults. When we adults meet a gossipy person, we sometimes feel a little uneasy or distrustful: "Do they talk about us, too?" When we show, by example, an unloving attitude toward others, our children get that uneasy, questioning feeling: "Am I part of that 'unloved' group Mom's talking about?"

*Attention* can help to further dispel those "unloved" feelings. Turn off the television, and listen to your child. When cooking, you can save your worries or preoccupation with the bills for later in the evening, and hear all about your child's day at school. We adults can often find many, many items to capture our attention: cooking, cleaning, paying bills, balancing checkbooks, making "important" telephone calls, or worrying about an endless list of matters. By turning your attention to your child, you can show that he or she is worth your time, even when that time is limited.

You cannot be an ideal parent, nor can you try to "make up for" the reality of your divorce. But you can live for the now and the future with your child. Seek that new closeness that is not only possible but also amazingly simple to achieve. Use your time with your child as positive, growing moments for your child — and yourself.

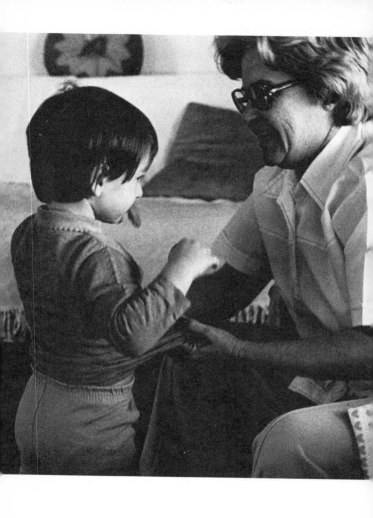

# CHAPTER 3

# The Adoptive or Unmarried Parent

When we think of single parenthood, we usually think of parents who have lost a husband or a wife through death, or have been divorced or separated. But there is a third kind of situation: when you're a single parent through adoption, or when you're an unmarried mother who has decided to raise your child.

## The Unmarried Natural Parent

For the unmarried mother, there is a stage to go through which is similar to the bereavement that follows the death of a spouse, or the period of anguish that follows a divorce. It is the *decision period,* and it can be just as difficult a period as that following death or divorce for other single parents. Getting through that decision period and coming out a whole person will take time, kindness, and much support—from parents, relatives, friends, church, or social agency. The central question, if you are in the decision period, is: "What shall I do?" It is a question that has no easy, general answer. So much depends on your circumstances: your age, financial status, and your personal aspirations are probably the three most critical. When faced with this decision, seek out those who have shown their love and care for you over a long period of time. Perhaps your parents might not be supportive; they might even be hostile. Or they may be so set in their ways that there is no right way but theirs. Seek out a close aunt, uncle, or friend; be with those who care more about you and your child, and less about imposing their particular point of view on you.

If you decide to raise your child, avoid the critics who might feel that you are "blinded by love" for your child, or that "your heart rules your head." I am not saying that you should rush headlong into a hasty decision, but, especially with parenthood, we need *more* of those feelings from the heart, and fewer so-called "socially correct" decisions.

Fortunately, we've learned that mothers can't (and won't) rush to get married anymore just because they think "it's the right thing to do," any more than a widow would *avoid* marriage because "it's the wrong thing to do."

You need *support* during your decision period; you don't need to be told what to do. Give yourself time. Think about what you want your life to be like . . . with your child. Or without your child. But, above all, make it *your decision*.

## The Single Adoptive Parent

More and more single men and women are seeking to adopt children, and they are increasingly successful as attitudes and laws become more flexible. It is a happy, even wonderful, situation, for their single parenthood is borne out of a willingness to give and receive love.

If you are a single parent who has adopted a child, you are to be applauded for the human, guiding touch you have placed into your adopted child's life. If there were only more like you to share themselves with our parentless children!

If you are single and contemplating adopting a child, you might have some doubts ranging from "Can I do it with my income?" to "How well will he or she adjust to my life, my rules?"

Granted, there are single parents who should not have adopted children. But the number of parents in that category is not as large as might be thought. If you are thinking of adopting, and you recognize the limitations with which you are working, I suggest you confer with an adoption agency and follow their advice. Explain your situation, income, and present family structure, but do emphasize the love you are able to give. Remember, different agencies have different standards, so if you are turned down by one, find out why. If they are so selective that you need to be a millionaire to adopt, try another agency that will place more emphasis on the love you have to give than on the things you can't. Let nothing stop you if you feel prepared to take on this responsibility. Recognize the impact you can make on a child's life. The writer George Eliot in saying, "a bachelor's children are always young," meant, I'm sure, that children keep adopted mothers and fathers young, too. What is the very next word after the word "adopt" in my pocket dictionary? "Adorable!"

# CHAPTER 4
# When You're a
# Single Mother

Among the countless expectations placed on
you as a single mother, it is likely that the central,
most important expectation is that you "pull your
life together." A divorce or a husband's death has
changed, disrupted, and altered your life to a great
degree. Divorce and death are anything but "minor
setbacks"; they can be wrenching, almost devastating blows. But you know that. And you have probably gone past much of the original grief, crying,
and fears. The hurt never seems to fully disappear,
but you are now able to start thinking of the future
—today and tomorrow.

As you look to the future, it is normal to feel a
lack of support, a support that, to one extent or another, was there before you became a single mother.
Whatever emotional, psychological, and even financial support you receive, it just isn't the same. It is
either gone entirely or changed so drastically that
you are not even certain as to how to begin "pulling
your life together" again. You simply don't have
another person to rely on to help share the job of being a parent. Since most single mothers work, it is a
real problem finding time not only for your children, but for yourself as well—time to be yourself

without being totally exhausted. Even for the most well-organized mothers, "pulling your life together" is not a simple, quick task.

To get perhaps a different perspective on the situation, let's consider, for a moment, your pre-single parent state, the time you were with your husband as a married pair. To one extent or another, all of the responsibilities, worries, tasks, and day-to-day jobs that had to be done were done by either you or your husband. Some were shared, but, if we think about it, much of the time spent by married persons is really spent alone. For example, the husband is at work, and the wife is at work or at home. Or, both are home, but the wife is balancing the checkbook and the husband is reading. Sometimes, the husband minds the kids while the wife is out bowling. The point is this: Most of the jobs or roles were pretty clear-cut—husband does this, and wife does that.

Having clear-cut roles and obligations in marriage is extremely convenient. When your husband left for work in the morning, you knew that a salary would be earned, thus providing income for the family. Your spouse might have had a similar expectation: He *knew* that the household jobs were going to be done. Regardless of some variations depending upon your particular relationship with your husband, it was a convenient arrangement.

Obviously, there is much more to marriage than convenience, but the hardest part of being a single mother is the inconvenience in your day-to-day life—of being faced with the problem of running a home and supporting children at the same time. Certainly you have emotional and sexual needs that may or may not have been adequately met in your marriage. But whether your marriage was happy, unhappy, or miserable, it was, to one extent or

33

another, convenient in the sense of sharing roles that are not being shared any longer. It will be difficult not to let the inconvenience, now a part of your life, interfere with your job as a single mother. It won't be simple; it will be trying, but not impossible. You are a mother, and your children need you now more than ever before, whether they are living with you or with your former husband.

You can take comfort from the fact that thousands of women are facing the same situation you face. In past years, being a single mother was probably more difficult, since only the father was seen as the rightful head of a family, and, when women attempted to fill that role, they met with trouble and frustration at every turn. Being a single mother today involves far less "static" from our culture. Despite the many problems you may have, both attitudes and conditions have improved considerably toward and for single women and single mothers. But simply because conditions today are more fair and equitable for single women, it doesn't follow that your life will now be a breeze. Improved attitudes toward your situation do not mean it is automatically a snap living with and raising children alone. Sure, it's easier now for a woman to get credit, but buying a new car is not, in itself, going to make a big difference in the way you live with your children. Your friendly bank might be an "equal opportunity lender," but you hardly need a mortgage.

In short, these advantages do not really help all that much when you are faced with the fact that you're a single mother. And that means that those very special people in your life need you much more than you need instant credit. Your children are special, and your children make you that special woman called mother.

What are your real needs at this time? Given the fact that you have full responsibility for running the home, given that you now have to deal directly with your children at all times, what steps can you take that will have a positive, healthy impact on your life and your children's lives?

## Don't Try to Be the "Ideal" Mother

Special? Yes, you're special. But ideal? It's just a myth. Milton R. Sapirstein, in *Paradoxes of Everyday Life*, said it well: "The ideal mother, like the ideal marriage, is a fiction." Bringing up children is no simple "hearts and flowers" proposition, and you must accept the fact that there are times you feel bad, angry, or miserable: times you feel far less than perfect. Sure, we all strive to improve ourselves, and when we set specific goals, nothing feels better than achieving them. But when we set the totally unattainable goal of being an ideal parent, we are just setting ourselves up for a letdown with a thick coating of guilt.

## Establish Your Authority as a Single Parent

If you are divorced, cooperation with your former spouse is terribly important, but not to the point where you rely on him to be the only authority figure, or to "be the bad guy." It won't work; it never does. Because if you rely on someone else to be the enforcer of your rules, you have no real authority at all. It is quite possible that being an authority figure is not your "natural" role, especially if your former husband did most of the disciplining. In the past, if you relied on him to do the dirty work ("Wait till your father gets home!"), take the bull by the horns *now* and accept your rightful role as a single parent. Children need and want structure and appreciate having limits set, whether they live in a single parent home or not.

It might be difficult at first for you to rely totally on yourself, and the temptation to leniency might be great. But, ask yourself: if you are not in charge when you're a single parent, who is?

The most essential task in establishing yourself as an authority figure is to learn the art of saying "no." As a single mother, the temptation to say "yes" to your child as a means of compensating will be a strong one. But resist it. For one thing, your finances are probably not in their best shape at this time, and children's requests can get constant and are often expensive. Another more important reason is that it is vital for children to understand that there are times when they must get — and accept — a "no" answer. Saying "no" should mean just that. Problems crop up when your child learns that your "no" *really* means "maybe," or "if-you-bother-me-long-enough-I'll-say-yes." You can't rely on anyone else to enforce your authority, be it your former spouse, a teacher, or the family physician. Recognize the likelihood that you are placing yourself in the role of a monitor or a baby-sitter with no power of your own if you relinquish your authority as parent. Say "no" when you feel it is necessary, feel no guilt about it, and make it short, sweet, and firm.

If your child is not accustomed to your authority, it's likely that, for starters, you will be confronted with "But Mom, why not?"; "You don't love me!"; "Daddy used to let me"; "You're not fair; or countless variations on the theme. Hold fast, because these are challenges. Don't get into an argument if you are confronted by such challenges — it's the worst thing to do. You have to live with your children, and you certainly don't want to live with day-after-day arguments.

You are going to be challenged. Fine. Steel yourself, get through this stage, and you're home free. Because if your child understands (and *believes*) that Mom is serious and will not back down, in a relatively short period of time (depending on his or her age and will power), your child will come to accept your "no." Just make sure that when you say "no," it is a sincere, thought-out answer. Avoid making excuses (Because I said so; Because I have no money; Because . . ."), but you can offer an explanation. For example: "I must say 'no,' John. When you calm down, I'd like to tell you why." It takes patience, certainly, but when you think about it, it's really the only way to live in harmony. If you respond to empty threats ("I want to live with Daddy"; "If Daddy were here you wouldn't do this!"), then you are probably going to be manipulated every time you try to exercise your authority.

Along with learning how to say "no," remember to include many "yes" answers. Keep in mind that a "yes" is a promise and needs to be followed through just as a "no" answer. Even if it means a hardship for you, once you have said "yes," stick to it. In exercising your authority, "yes" and "no" are powerful words. Use them well; use them carefully, firmly, and, always, lovingly.

## Make Time for Your Children and Yourself

A major, everyday barrier to a harmonious single parent home is the real problem of time. You love your children; you want to be with them, but you "can't find the time." When you are a single mother, the chances are great that you have a full-time job (in addition to being a full-time home-maker and full-time mother). You are *tired* when you come home in the evening. And your son needs help with his homework; your daughter needs help with her slacks. Or the dishes are unwashed; the dog is howling to be walked; and all you feel like doing is diving into bed for that wonderful invention — sleep!

There are some practical steps you can take in trying to find time at home to spend on yourself and with your children. First, divide up the work at home. If your children are older than three years of age, start making clear what their jobs are. Chapter Seven has some suggestions as to how you can make your home run more smoothly by enlisting your children's assistance.

Second, do not expect to find time, because it can't be found. You must make it and take it. Just as you will need to look closely at some of the jobs to be done around the house, consider also some alternatives to your job schedule outside the home. Can you reduce your work hours without taking too much of a financial loss? Can you adjust your work hours to suit your children's school schedule? Could you consider taking different, less time-consuming employment?

If your answers are all "no," then consider how you use the free time you now have. Are you spending time at home doing things — out of habit — that you really never wanted to do and certainly don't need to do now — like shining crystal or silver that is rarely used, like waxing the floor because you've always done it once a week? Start eliminating these time-wasters that might have lost their meaning. Postpone the jobs that are important but can wait. Because your time is precious, you want to spend it on people, not things. And the people who really need your time and energy are you and your children. Love your neighbor, but don't worry about her opinion of your floor or silver. Enjoy television, but don't let it make you think your time should be spent pulling dazzling white masterpieces from your washer. Love your children, and never let anyone make you feel that anything else is more important.

# CHAPTER 5
# When You're a
# Single Father

Just as a woman is expected to "pull her life back together" after a divorce or being widowed, men, too, find their lives just as disrupted and in need of that same "pulling together." That "pulling together" can be a particularly difficult job when you're a single father.

For example, the single father can no longer rely on another person to help share the workload that comes with being a parent. You no longer have the luxury of sharing with another adult the responsibility of parenting. Many find this lack of support and cooperation almost overwhelming. If, before you became a single father, you were not directly involved in meeting your child's needs on a day-to-day basis, it is as if, all of a sudden, you are expected to learn the art of child raising in record-breaking time. Even for fathers experienced in the art and science of child rearing, adjusting to the role of a single father is anything but a snap.

Due to changing attitudes toward men and fatherhood, there are some real indications that being a single father today does not necessarily mean being "left out" or "playing second fiddle." In fact, over half a million families in the United States are headed by single fathers. Custody arrangements no longer blindly favor the mother, and more and more men are willing (and able) to take on greater parental responsibility whether they have child custody or not.

How well are those men who comprise the statistics doing as single fathers? What do they feel is their greatest difficulty?

Some of the most recent research into single fatherhood shows that the hardest part of being a single father is balancing work (career) with responsibilities as a parent. Unlike single mothers, the single father does not report as great a difficulty in establishing himself as an authority figure. But many men feel (some very intensely) that they are inadequate parents. They find it unsettling to suddenly be confronted with the real problem of dealing directly with their children and not "through another person." Most of the men say that they feel as if they really never knew their children as people. Being a single father has forced them to be with, and deal with, their children on a one-to-one, "Hello, stranger, let's get to know each other," basis. This is probably the most healthy and positive outcome of the single father's predicament: getting to really know his own children. No less an authority than DaVinci, writing his *Notebooks* five hundred years ago, said: "Nothing can be loved or hated unless it is first known." The single father can, through this getting-to-know-you process, learn to love his children as real persons needing his time and attention. In short, being a single father can bring you closer to your children.

This particular aspect of single fatherhood really came into focus at a recent conference I had at my school with a divorced mother. She complained to me about her former husband's weekend visits with their daughter. She said that her daughter, Jessica, felt "bored" doing things with her father. Jessica claimed, "We don't even say very much to each other. I just sit in the car until we get someplace." Mother asked me if I thought it was a "good idea" for Jessica to keep seeing her dad, since they never seemed to communicate when together. My response was that perhaps Dad didn't *know* his daughter well enough to even have a conversation that would last longer than a minute or two, and that the time they were now spending together was probably the most important time in their lives. It was Dad's first chance to try to learn about Jessica as a person, and vice-versa. Some weeks later, Mother came by the school to help with the Brownie troop and happened to mention in passing that things were "much better" between her daughter and her former husband. They just needed some time to get to know each other.

There is no question that being a single father can be a difficult role. Most single fathers desperately want to continue to be wonderful and special people in their children's lives, but find it very hard given their added responsibilities.

Regardless of the legal complications, if you have been through a divorce or the wrenching experience of losing your wife through death, you can continue to be that very special person to your children. To make your father-child relationship as wonderful and rewarding as possible, it will help to look at your role as a single father from two points of view: your children's needs and your needs.

## Your Children's Needs

Of the many needs that growing children have, none comes anywhere near the need for nurture. It is the single most important aspect of human life. Parents have always been told to love their children, to feel love toward them. But to *show love* — that's a different issue. In general, men have rarely been given the opportunity to learn how to nourish growth, to nurture children. What we have been taught is what I call (for lack of a better word) *custodial* tasks, and, unfortunately, these custodial tasks often get mistaken for real nurture.

It is important to note the difference between custodial behavior (I don't mean child custody) and nurture. The necessary tasks which can be done by you, or a baby-sitter, or Aunt Sarah are custodial. These range from changing diapers and taking a child's temperature to enrolling a child in school or attending a graduation. These are all necessary tasks; they are routine jobs that can be done by anyone reasonably competent in the ways of child care. You, as a single father, might have to learn how to do some of these custodial tasks. But they are of far less importance to your child's well-being than the need your child has for your nurture.

The special nurture that only dads can provide consists of a whole lot more than mere custodial tasks. A father's nurture consists of a constant supply of special, loving moments in a child's life.

They must be loving. "You can't teach them unless you reach them" is an old axiom that applies here. Your child cannot possibly know of your love unless you show it. Your child cannot read your mind. You seem upset, for example, and you know why you're upset. You had a bad day at work. But, your child takes it personally. ("What did I do now, Dad?" your child might silently question.) This simply means that you have to be conscious of the messages you are sending when you're with your child.

I mentioned "attending a graduation" as a custodial task. Anyone can attend a graduation ceremony. But what makes that task special (and nurturing) is the sincere, human hug of pride, happiness, and love that only a parent can give. At times, loving moments must be physical: a hug, a kiss, or being picked up and placed on your shoulders. Loving moments can be as simple as a wink of the eye, or as involved as a father-and-daughter dance.

They have to be *special*. Special does not mean that every time you see your child you must have the most interesting day planned. Nor does it mean a lavish gift or toy as a present. Gifts, toys, and attractive places to go are fun, but they can be gotten from anyone. What then is "special" about what you can give? Yourself. Special is that glow of joy on your face when you see your child. Special is holding your child's hand when you are walking to the restaurant from the car. Special is not getting angry over a "bad" report card, but letting your child know you care that the next one will be better. And special is listening to what your son or daughter has to say, talking to him or her as a real person, giving the same attention you'd give a customer in your store, your boss in the office, or your friend who needs advice.

Finally, nurture needs to be *constant*. Those special, loving moments just cannot happen sporadically, only when you're in a good mood. Nurture needs to be a pattern developed between parent and child. In an inconsistent world, every child needs his or her father to be stable; you just can't turn off your loving feelings when you feel "down." All fathers, single or married, have only a limited time to be with their children. Make that time a time of nurture.

## Your Needs

There is little question that your children's needs are important, especially when you're a single parent. Your children are dependent people; their needs can only be met through and with you. However, as a single father, there is only one person who can really help you meet your needs. And that person is you.

As a single father, you have two basically different kinds of needs: personal needs (such as a need for friendship, love, and emotional fulfillment) and parental needs (those needs that are a part of your role as a parent). In Chapter Nine there are suggestions to help you meet your personal needs. For now, let's focus on the four most common parental needs expressed by a majority of single fathers:

- Working, and finding time for your children,
- Dealing with younger children,
- Handling the routine, custodial tasks, and,
- Avoiding the "both mother and father" and "ideal parent" traps.

There are no absolute answers to the four problems outlined above. Every situation is different. But, if you are a single father, you've most likely been confronted with at least one of the four problem areas. Some of the following ideas may help you work with an inconvenient (but not impossible) situation.

## Working, and Finding Time for Your Children

We really don't have much of a choice when it comes to working. The best attitude to take is an accepting one, glad that we have jobs or careers at all!

Whether or not you like your job is certainly important, but it is not the issue here. What is at stake is finding time for your children. Most single fathers have no argument with the need to hold a job, with working as such, but resent the fact that it so often leaves them drained and too tired to adequately meet other needs.

Take a close look at your employment. Regardless of your particular job or title, ask yourself this first and rather important question: "How much of my job do I bring home with me?" Think about and determine, for example, whether or not you bring home paperwork that doesn't really have to be done at home, or whether or not you have "work on your mind" when you are home.

Count the hours you spend at your place of employment and involved with work you've taken home. How many hours per week? Add these hours to your sleeping, eating, and other necessary time, and what's left over? Two hours a day? Three?

If so, it is time to draw the line! No job — absolutely no job — is worth it if your time with your children is being infringed upon by that job.

We often hear people say "I just can't find the time" to do what are considered important tasks in parenting. Time cannot be found unless you look for it, and it will never be found unless you make it! There is a big difference between trying to find time and actually making it.

With daycare facilities in abundance, it is often easy for a single father with custody to simply call the center to say that he'll be one, two, or even three hours late in picking up his child. Unless it is a real emergency, try to avoid the temptation to view routine tasks as being more important than taking time for your child. Or, if your children are older and home by themselves, don't take advantage of the fact that "they're responsible." Make time to be with them, and guard it jealously.

## Handling Young Children

We have all heard the sayings about how important "a mother's love" is to a child. But Moliere spoke up for fathers when he wrote in *Don Juan*: "How easily a father's tenderness is recalled . . ." A father's tenderness can touch the life of an adolescent, a preschooler, and even an infant. Many single fathers, feeling at a loss when confronted with their preschool children, think that they can step in when the children are older. Or they honestly feel that their influence is not needed; the child is somehow "not aware" of the father. Not so!

What to do with a younger child? Anything at all! Playing a simple game like rolling a ball, giving piggy-back rides, playing peek-a-boo, or even watching "Sesame Street" together are some of the many things to do with a preschooler.

If you have custody of a preschool child, or if you are a widower, and you are short on ideas for your free time together, then adapt routine household chores so you can do them with your youngster. Learn from mothers or other fathers what they do with their preschoolers. Ask the nursery school or daycare teacher for suggestions.

If your former wife has custody of your pre-

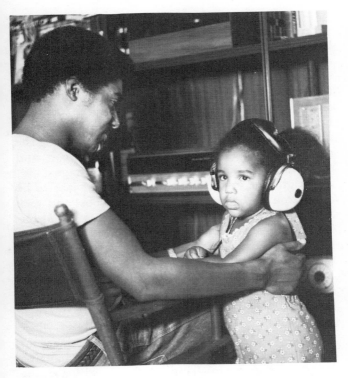

school child, you need to be with him or her just as much as with older children—maybe even more. Younger children are not the special province of mothers.

## Handling the Routine, Custodial Tasks

I use the word "custodial" not in the sense of a parent with custody, but to describe the thousands of maintenance tasks a parent must perform for a child or with a child. They are those routine jobs that are needed to keep a household going and a child growing.

49

For the single father with custody, or for the widowed father, the child's day is usually occupied by school. Problems, however, can crop up in the evening. Some research suggests that single fathers tend to be more permissive with their children after the experience of a divorce or a death. Remember that your children need firm limits around the house, and now more than ever, their help is needed. If, for example, you find yourself doing the dishes, dumping the trash, cleaning the floor, and doing all the laundry, and you have a teenage child, stop right there. Establish a schedule of jobs to be done around the house (include your jobs) and stick to it. Make it a written schedule and post it in a conspicuous place. Avoid letting yourself become a "slave" to your child to somehow "make up for" the fact that you are a single father.

If your former wife has custody, the chances are that custodial tasks are pretty much taken care of by her. But when you are with your child, there is nothing to prevent you from doing those "little things" which are vitally important: checking your child's appearance, fixing your son's tie, or changing the baby's diaper are all custodial tasks with a strong undercurrent of nurture.

## Avoiding the "Both Mother and Father" and "Ideal Parent" Traps

Avoid getting into these binds by doing away with the idea that you must somehow compensate your child for the loss or separation that has occurred. If you are a widower, nothing you do, wish, or pay for will replace your loss. If you're a single father with custody or a widower, you need not worry about the mythical "woman's touch." Yes, you will have more work to do, and maybe that work will involve tasks that your wife did, but keep in mind that you simply cannot be two people. The most important thing you can give your son or daughter is your example as a positive, warm, and loving human being. Children neither need nor want more than that.

Remind yourself that many, many children have grown up to lead happy and healthy lives, despite the fact that their mothers were deceased, absent, or "part time." What matters is the person who is there, not the person who is absent. If, when you are present with your child, you're there as one your child can rely on, you've made it. Even if you cannot be with your child as frequently as you might wish, you can make those hours together have a strong impact on your child's future.

The "ideal parent" and "perfect father" are mythical creatures. No child has ever had an "ideal father," and, if you think about it, no normal child would even want one. Think about your own father —even his weaknesses and the ways he sometimes felt let down in life. Did those drawbacks make him any less precious to you?

CHAPTER 6
# Role Models for
# Your Children

Most single parents, men or women, seem greatly concerned with the question: "How can I provide a good model for my child? I can't be both man and woman. What can I do?"

A single father with a daughter is concerned with the fact that a female influence (role model) is missing in his daughter's day-to-day life. A single father with a son somehow feels that a "mother's influence" is missing. The situation is the same for a single mother: her son is without a male influence, her daughter "lacks a father figure."

Unfortunately, our society has a number of expressions that add to our insecurity in this matter: "A strong male figure," "A woman's touch," "A man around the house," "Daddy's little girl," and hundreds of other cliches that often serve more to haunt than to help us.

An important distinction must be made between sex role models and human role models.

- Sex Role Models—Where we hold that an adult of the same sex is important for a child's growth (such as father for son, mother for daughter).

- Human Role Models—Where we believe that the actual sex of the person seen as role model is less important than the person himself or herself.

## Sex Role Models

There is no doubt that certain words have particular connotations or special meanings. Let's take the words "man" and "masculine." Man. Some people tend to think of a particular person right away—a former husband, a first boyfriend, or Burt Reynolds. Or, others might form a more general concept when hearing the word: smoking a pipe, an easy chair, someone who pays the bills, or working with a circular saw in the workshop.

Now let's consider the words "woman" and "feminine." When we hear "woman," we might think of a particular person: our mother, a certain girlfriend, or Lindsay Wagner. Others might think along less specific lines. "Woman" to them might connote housework, scrubbing floors and ears, or doing the shopping. So, what we think of as being implied by the word "man" and the word "woman" can differ rather greatly. These are sex role models. If you are a father, and you want your daughter to learn a suitable sex role but there is no woman she can use as a sex role model, all you need to do is to teach her that women wash floors, cook, clean houses and ears, and should grow up to look like Lindsay Wagner. If you are a single mother, and you want your son to learn a suitable sex role, all you need do is teach your son that men smoke pipes, sit in easy chairs, pay bills, make wooden objects in a shop, and grow up to look like Burt Reynolds. If you find this a bit hard to take (and I hope you do!), take a look at *Human Role Models*.

## Human Role Models

Again, let's think of the word "man." This time, however, omit the things that our culture has told us men are supposed to do. Get rid of the pipe smoke, the easy chair, and all the rest of the clutter. What positive words and feelings now come to mind when you hear the word "man"? Warm, loving, gentle, giving, caring, and protective. Now think of the word "woman." Just as with "man," let's get rid of those words that supposedly tell us what women are, or what they are supposed to do: housekeeping, sweeping, and all the rest. Now, what positive words come to mind when the word "woman" is spoken? Warm? Yes. Gentle and giving? Definitely. Loving, caring, and protective? Absolutely! *These terms— whether they apply to a man or to a woman—are human role model terms*. In short, they are words that can be used with either sex, because they describe real humans. Real people love. Real people care. Real people are gentle, giving, and protective. No matter whether you are talking about a man or a woman, these human qualities are the important bases for role modeling.

The whole question of role models really pertains to the larger question: "What do we want our children to do with their lives?" When we try to give them sex role models, maybe we are trying to teach them the wrong things. Do we really want our daughters to grow up and do all the things our culture expects of them? Do we really want our sons to grow up and do all the things our culture says are acceptable? Must our daughters become housewives in order to show us that they have had "acceptable role models"? Should our sons feel compelled to cut wood, hunt for animals, whistle at women, or play baseball just because that's what our culture expects of men? Of course not! Now there is nothing wrong if a child, boy or girl, chooses to play baseball, wash dishes, clean a house, or hunt. But it is wrong if we think a child by virtue of being male or female is supposed to do these things. As a single parent you need to be alert to whether or not you are conveying those "culturally expected" messages to your child.

Do you expect your son to "take it like a man"? If so, you need to look again at what you want your child to be when he or she grows up. Try concentrating on human role model words and actions, on human stereotypes rather than sex stereotypes.

"Doesn't a boy need a father? A girl need a mother?" Fathers and mothers are wonderful people. But, even more than a father or a mother, a child needs a warm, loving, caring human being. That human being, regardless of sex, will be a far more effective role model than having a man around the house just because he's a man, or having a woman around the house just because she's a woman. There is no way to compensate for the loss of a father or a mother. I know, because, as a youngster, I lost my father, and I was raised by a single parent.

Don't make the mistake of using "your child's need for a sex role model" as an excuse for remarriage. If you wish to remarry, fine. If you don't, that's fine, too. But avoid considering marriage "for the kid's sake." If you are considering remarriage, you must take into account the fact that you do have a child. But to consider marriage even in part because your child needs it is an error. Your child doesn't. The person whom your son or daughter really needs is you.

Your child needs you as a human role model. Teach him or her that—whether he's a boy or she's a girl, whether you are a man or a woman—there are certain important human qualities that he or she must have to truly be successful. You cannot ever be "both father and mother," and there is no need for you to try to do so. By simply being a caring, gentle, loving human being, you will be providing your son or daughter with a foundation that will support them well in later life.

Even if you believe that men and women must act differently, remember that if your son or daughter is physically well, and you provide him or her with those important human values, you can rest assured that he or she will not suffer "sex identity" problems. A son can be taught by his mother to respect himself and show respect to others. He can be taught by your example that respect for others is a fine form of love. Your daughter need not learn that women "must be submissive" and "listen to and obey" men. She can be taught to demand respect from others and to respect herself as well.

Clarissa Start, author of the excellent book *When You're a Widow*, speaks of how, after her husband died, she realized that she and her son were able to function well, even in areas she had thought would need her husband's guiding hand.

## Outside Help

Girl Scouts, Boy Scouts, 4-H Clubs, Future Farmers of America are all great organizations. There is no doubt that your child, boy or girl, needs to learn from others the same age. Likewise, he or she does need the different viewpoint a teacher, scoutmaster, or den mother can provide. But never delude yourself into thinking that they can somehow give more than you, that they can be better role models than you. Free your mind of sex role stereotypes and plunge into the business of giving what you've already got, the qualities of the human spirit that will make your child a real man or woman.

# CHAPTER 7
# You and Your Child at Home

If most parents, single or married, could pick the two concerns that dominate their lives as parents, it's almost a sure bet they would pick home and children. Running the home and raising well-behaved children can be even more pressing when you are a single parent, mostly because the workload can no longer be divided between two adults.

## Managing the Home

Running a household can be dreadfully boring at times. All the routine tasks can boil down to drudgery. On the other hand, we know that few things in life can give us the satisfaction that a warm, well-kept residence gives. Whether it is an apartment in the city or a home in the country, it's *home*.

Even if a home is comfortable and warm, no one can enjoy being home if it is a constant struggle.

Especially if you're a single parent, struggling through each day's chores can make you want to say, "It's just not worth it." There are some practical, useful suggestions that might help make your home life run a bit more smoothly. Begin by taking a look at your particular circumstances to recognize and identify what you'd like to change. The following suggestions might be helpful especially if you're a newly-single parent.

• **Get Help at Home if You Need It.** The sometimes sudden adjustment necessary for the single parent can be overpowering. If your income allows, hire help (a person to clean, for example) for the first few weeks or months. If your income will not allow this luxury, look to local governmental agencies that might have part-time help available for low-income single mothers or fathers. If your income or convictions will allow neither choice, there is all the more reason to utilize your children's help, especially if they are older children. Set up a schedule for yourself and the children, and stick to it. Divide up the work fairly, and try not to feel guilty in doing so. It can be very beneficial to them to have to face up to their responsibilities when it comes to routine chores.

• **Reassess Your Standards.** Now that you're a single parent, think again about the way you want your home to be. When you were married, your standards were not identical to your spouse's standards, and it is entirely possible that you adopted, or adapted to, his or her standards. Change those habits, standards, or expectations that right now, today, don't meet your needs or the needs of your children. In a sense, you are starting from scratch, so try to please yourself. For example, if your former spouse was a "stickler" for detail around the house and you're not, suit yourself. If you don't like house-plants, get rid of them. In short, readjust your home and the standards by which it is run to suit your own criteria.

• **Keep Up Your Expectations of Your Children.** A common tendency among single parents is to ease up on the expectations they place on their children. Don't try to compensate your children for the loss or separation of parents, because it just is not possible to replace a person with an object or a more-lenient attitude. If you think that your children have "been through enough already," that's understandable. But it does not mean that you need to make their life duty-free from now on.

If you present routine responsibilities around the house as punishment, children will learn to resent their duties. Instead, try to help your children view their chores as "no big deal" duties which are a natural part of their contribution to the home. You are particularly vulnerable now that you're a single parent, but do try to remain unswayed if you're confronted with, "You're being unfair . . . you're a slave driver now that Dad's (Mom's) not here . . . ," or a thousand other variations.

Keep the fact of your widowhood or divorce separate from your duties as a parent. Be matter-of-fact: "I'm sorry you feel that way, but there's work to be done." If you pick up their slack, chances are excellent that you will find yourself doing more and more of their work. You have been through so much already, you hardly need to become a slave to your children. If you insist on their cooperation, they will eventually be able to do more and more toward carrying out their responsibilities with less and less supervision from you.

• **Maintain Reasonable Home Expectations.**

61

While you should keep your expectations high and insist that your children accept responsibilities, the other side of the coin is to be reasonable. Reasonable tasks, if presented in a positive manner, give children chances to feel important. Rather than feel "put upon," children with jobs to do at home often enjoy the responsibility. Younger children can do literally hundreds of jobs around the house such as watering plants, matching socks in the laundry, tending to pets, making beds, caring for a small garden, washing and/or drying dishes, and many, many others. There is no shortage of jobs around the home for young children and teenagers alike. The important thing is to be reasonable in your expectations. Requiring a teenager to pick up things in his or her room and keep it neat is reasonable. Requiring that it be kept immaculate is unreasonable. Similarly, having a five-year-old water plants is reasonable. Getting upset when they've been flooded out is unreasonable. Instead, demonstrate how to water plants and be realistic in expecting the child to make mistakes.

• **Don't Expect Perfection.** Your child is willing to do his or her share of the work around the house. Fine. The work is reasonable. You've seen to that. But remember that nothing can kill the joy of doing a task—no matter how simple or how complex—nothing can kill the fun or challenge as quickly as demands for perfection. As in the above example, the five-year-old will, occasionally, flood the philodendron. So what? A simple reminder is enough.

We adults make a mistake when, just because we've said something once, we think it becomes engraved in stone. "How many times have I told you . . . " is the classic statement. Avoid it, because—yes—you will have to repeat. Your children are people like us adults. I know that I would not want my physician to scream at me whenever I visit him: "How many times have I told you to lose twenty pounds?" Be reasonable!

A good rule of thumb to use as to when to demand compliance is this: If your child's safety or the safety of another person is involved, don't feel bad about laying it on heavy. For example, my daughter received a firm, clear warning when she was four about being in the street alone. When she darted out again into the street, her bottom was warmed. I didn't repeat my words, because action was necessary. Nor did I scream: "How many times have I told you . . . " because the potential for serious injury was too real.

However, the vast majority of parental warnings or threats do not revolve around serious danger situations, but are for relatively minor, but usually annoying, actions. Put your parental concern into perspective by resolving to hold your heavy hand for the really serious threats to your child's (or another person's) well-being. Getting angry over the flooding of houseplants, or over a broken dinner plate, just isn't worth the hurt feelings and possible distance it places between you and your child.

## Sex Education and the Single Parent

Our greatest difficulties in sex education do not arise from the natural necessity of telling our children about the reproductive process, but from the artificial educational dictate that we keep "sex education" separate as a scientific body of knowledge from all other aspects of the human loving experience. Nobody ever seems happy with the sex education courses taught in the schools. I see two reasons for the disenchantment. First, the courses fall flat due to their too-general scope, according to some parents. Or, second, some (the other group) think there should be no sex education courses whatsoever. The truth is that a really meaningful sex education simply cannot be "taught" like multiplication by an institution, but can be learned by children from adults closest to them. Schools can teach words, terms, and processes, but in order for sex to mean more than a mechanical operation, it needs to be handled by someone (like you!) who can relate the "facts" to human loving.

A parent can turn a potentially unpleasant job into a wonderful opportunity to help a child see the relationship between sex and human loving. To a teacher of sex education in school, it's a job. To a parent, it's an opportunity.

• **Encourage Your Child to Ask Questions.** Even if you do not know the answer, don't ignore the question. In responding to your child, use proper names for parts of the body, and avoid the "cute" words. You don't have to know all things, but you do need to allow your child to talk to you, to ask you what different words mean.

• **Create an Honest, Open Atmosphere.** This closeness is especially important when you are a single parent. If your child uses a vulgar word, give him or her a better, more acceptable word to replace it. Punishing a child for using a vulgar word is of no help to him or her. Remember that kids do eventually hear different words at school and play. They get double-meaning jokes from television, magazines, or newspapers. You are the best source your child has for honest and helpful information. You can give your child so much more than just facts and figures, which, depending on his or her age, can be frightening, boring, or just plain puzzling. Start sex education as soon as your child begins asking questions. There is just no way to suddenly teach a child about human sexuality when your daughter begins menstruation, or when your son begins shaving.

The human part of sex education has little to do with sex facts themselves, but revolves around trust, caring, and a sense of warmth that exists between you and your child. If your child can learn how to give, how to show love in a nonsexual way, he or she will be well prepared for sexual loving. Our kids need to know sexual facts, but without a context of human love for understanding these facts, they are, at best, confusing and, at worst, disgusting. By your example, you can instill those real, human values — by the way you talk to and about others, the way you show kindness, the way you hug, and the way you give of yourself. Knowledge of the physical facts of sex is only part of sex education. What makes it meaningful and complete is the child's psychological well-being nurtured by you throughout childhood and adolescence.

## Discipline and Behavior

As a parent, you have the responsibility for helping your children grow as healthy, well-behaved, happy, and effective human beings. Whether you have custody or not, developing good behavior in your children is a matter of keen concern. But you won't settle for just a "well-behaved, obedient child," because successful living demands much more. Society presents many, many options to our children — some not very pleasant and some downright harmful — and we want them to be prepared to make rational, positive choices, choices that will let their lives be successful, and choices that will keep them from physical or mental harm.

Wanting a good life for our children and helping them know how to achieve it are often two different matters. Development of skills for meaningful living starts in the home. Schools alone cannot instill the necessary qualities in children. Schools can help children learn important information about living, but parents must help children achieve control of themselves and develop the values and human qualities with which to productively use this information.

It's a pretty complex business bringing up children, and it can be more complicated when you are a single parent. But it is not impossible. You may have to make changes in the way you deal with your child, but you, as a single parent, can know the satisfaction of successful parenting. The following ideas and suggestions may be helpful.

• **Permit Trust to Grow between You and Your Child.** Trust is shown through actions and words. Look at your actions carefully. Do you go through your child's pockets looking for "heaven-knows-what"? Do you telephone the mother of your teenage daughter's friend just to make sure your daughter was telling the truth about her destination? Children very quickly pick up attitudes of distrust which can be devastating to a parent-child relationship.

Watch carefully what you say to your children. "I see that you're dating that tramp again behind my back" is hardly the way to help your teenage son trust you. Replace suspicion and sarcasm with caring. Even when you're upset, avoid trampling on your child's feelings. Building trust through your actions and words means that when something really important comes up, and you must know the truth, you can be certain that you'll get the truth.

• **Use Honest Praise, Lavishly.** No child ever became spoiled because of too much praise. Praise is a valid, effective way of showing love; all that's required is that it be sincere, and given when deserved. Whether it is for a good report card or a well-pitched little league game, praise works wonders. Constant reassurance is critical to a child's feeling good about himself or herself.

Don't wait for perfection before you praise. Praise a job well done, and don't expect your child to "do a perfect job."

• **Learn from Others.** Look at the ways other single parents relate to, and live with, their children. Notice the finer points of other parent-child relationships. Do other parents tend to yell? Talk softly? When you are with your children at the local burger palace, how do other parents deal with their kids? Don't be afraid to try to incorporate some of their techniques into your style of parenting. We can (and should) learn a great deal from other parents. Turn those talk sessions you have with other parents into real learning experiences for you. If you have had a problem with your child in a certain area, don't hesitate to share it with another adult you respect and trust. The odds are good that other parents have been through the same situation. Sometimes the best professional advice pales in comparison to the advice we get from other parents.

• **Test Yourself.** Try to become aware of the way your child behaves when you are not present. Find out how well your son behaves with the babysitter. Learn how well your daughter acts when she is with your former spouse. Is there a big difference? If you are constantly battling with your child at home, but the babysitter seems totally placid and pleased when you return, maybe something's wrong. Maybe

67

your child has you "pegged" and knows all your vulnerable spots.

If there is a real difference in behavior when your child is with your former spouse, work cooperatively—for the advantage of your child—to get your signals straight. Learn about your child's behavior in school, too. Teachers are often quite perceptive and can give valuable feedback on your child's behavior. Don't get defensive if their report is not what you would like to hear. Take any ideas and suggestions not as a personal insult, but as an honest attempt to help you live with your child—and vice-versa. Your child's teacher, a close friend, or even the den mother can provide excellent "second opinions" in your effort to raise well-behaved children. Ask them for their viewpoints, seek an understanding relationship with others who deal with your child, but never ask them to take over your job.

• **Reject the Misbehavior—Not the Child.** The relationship between child and single parent can become tense at times. Even small misdeeds can sometimes take on mammoth proportions. Keep your corrections aimed at the misbehavior—not at your child, his integrity, or her personality. For example, some parents get so furious that at times they'll say: "I can't stand you anymore! I hate you!" Angry words like these are especially taboo if yours is a single parent home, because your child has no second parent for reassurance, no immediate "out" or relief. Therefore, it is vital to keep the "love lines" open: correct the behavior ("I don't like what you've done, Steve"), but don't make it personal, a "me-against-you" battle. In a world that will give them much to battle about, make your home one of solace: an accepting, understanding, and placid one.

When the chips are really down, you've just

plain had it, and you're ready to explode, get away! Isolate yourself in another room, start washing the dishes—furiously—or scrub the floor. But don't tear into your child!

• **Don't Nag.** Learn to make the distinction between what your child needs and what your child wants. These are often confused by parents. Sometimes, what a child wants is something needed, but many times children get what they want without getting what they need.

For example. When I had dinner as a child, I would often ask for more of a certain dish. Often, I couldn't finish the extra helping I asked for and received. My father would tell me that my "eyes were bigger than my stomach," meaning that there was a difference between what I needed (maybe just a bite more) and what I wanted (a huge second helping).

In many situations, we see children getting what they want, and not what they need. One of the teachers at a local high school told me that his school served "junk food" to the students, and it really bothered him. Knowing that the high school had a very well-equipped kitchen, I asked why they could not get a decent hot lunch. He told me that the cafeteria tried balanced hot lunches three years ago, but "the kids didn't want them."

As parents, we must be careful to, first, be able to find out what our children need, and to do what we can to provide for those needs. Second, we should try to avoid letting wants dominate our parental decisions. Sure, your child should get some fun out of life—a frivolous toy never hurts—but, if we become led by the *wants* (this is similar to the "gimmes"), we can tend to think we're meeting *needs*.

As a single parent, ask yourself, "What does my

child need?" Does your son need that Tonka truck, or does he need understanding and a hug? Does your daughter need a whole slew of souvenirs from your trip to the zoo, or does she need only a smile from you? Try to keep the differences clear: *needs* versus *wants*.

• **Accept the Fact That Men Can Be Just as Effective Disciplinarians as Women.** And vice-versa. You simply cannot blame your possible failings in managing your children's behavior on your sex. It is normal to sometimes feel, "I wish there was a man (or woman) here to handle this problem." But such a feeling hints at self-pity and excuse-making which helps no one.

It is incorrect to believe, especially in today's world, that men are somehow less loving, less nurturing than women. The power to love and nurture children is within us regardless of sex. Whether you are a single father or a single mother, you can effectively give both loving nurture and firm disciplinary guidance to your children. Forget all the myths of a "woman's touch" or a "father's strong guidance." Single mothers can provide firm, correct structure to a child's behavior just as surely as a father can wrap his arms around his kids in an "I love you" hug of understanding.

• **Tell Your Children What Is Expected of Them.** The reason behind much of the unacceptable behavior we parents see is that children honestly don't know any better. Children very often don't know what is expected of them; they have either not yet learned or are not yet capable of learning what we adults expect. For example, the four-year-old child who innocently walks out of a supermarket with an unpaid item, the thirteen-year-old boy who uses his father's screwdriver as a chisel, or the toddler who eats five prize African violets is not being "bad." They have either made mistakes, or they have not yet learned about certain, adult standards.

You don't need to post a list of expectations or "thou shalt nots" on the living room wall, but you do need to, patiently, teach your child what is acceptable behavior and what is not acceptable. Take into account your child's age, ability to understand the rules, and the difference between deviant behavior and simply not knowing any better.

• **Never Ignore Misbehavior.** It is a mistake to think that unacceptable behavior will "disappear" on its own. There are some behaviors which are normal: A two-year-old child's "no" is not the same as a seven-year-old's "no." It is true that youngsters "go through stages," but don't deceive yourself into thinking that most or all misbehavior is just a stage your child is going through. Teenagers are often somewhat negative and rebellious, but vulgar, insulting language directed at you is not "a stage." Nor will your child "grow out of it." You must deal with it directly.

• **Be Fair.** Be fair about what you call acceptable behavior, using your judgment and common sense as your best guides. For example, to punish your child for a bad report card is probably not called for. Report cards are the result of many factors; there is usually nothing specifically "bad" that your child has done. But if your son's behavior at home and at school has been poor, that is the area to address. Focus on the child not doing assigned homework, not on the lack of academic achievement. Being fair means making the rules as clear as possible and ensuring that they are just.

• **Make the Punishment Fit the Crime.** When the established and understood rules are broken, it is time to punish. An example: Your son has been instigating some fights with other children. You have made it clear that fighting is not acceptable and that a particular punishment can be expected if the fighting continues. He knows the rule, and he knows what the punishment is. He deliberately fights. Your next step is to have him suffer the consequences of his misbehavior.

Your child needs to be accountable for his or her own behavior. In cases of deliberate misbehavior, it is crucial that you act, and act quickly. Develop a clear-cut rules and consequences system so that your child knows where you stand—a system that says: "If you break the rules, you will suffer the consequences." If your child learns that he or she will suffer those consequences, your child will soon learn that the personal acceptance of responsibility is a very important trait. It is the cornerstone of being in charge of yourself, of being able to make effective choices later in life. When your child is confronted with, for example, drugs or alcohol, he or she needs to be able to choose the beneficial, wise course of action. We make a tragic error of misguided love when we try to take the blame for what our children do. They must learn the consequences of their behavior, words, and actions, and that they and only they are responsible for them.

• **Don't Seek Emotional Compensation from Your Children.** When you are a single parent, there might be a temptation to lean on your children, seeking their support in place of that formerly given by your spouse. Despite their maturity, even older children just are not psychologically able to lend the support you might seek. Practically speaking, if you do lean on them too much, you might find your role as authority figure in serious jeopardy when the time

73

comes to "be the parent" again.

• **Encourage Development of Your Child's Talents.** You don't need to drive your children to music, ballet, art, or drama lessons every day of the week, but do seek ways to develop confident, competent children. So many adults find that, when they are in their late teens or early twenties, there is little special in their lives: they feel rather incompetent. Parents—consciously or unconsciously—sometimes put down their children and their abilities in ways harmful to the child's needed sense of competency. We should not try to raise cocky, overly self-assured kids, but I do think we should consider our children's future needs. They will need to be good at something, to feel that there are at least some important things they can do well. Praise, reassurance, understanding, and old fashioned moral support go a long way toward instilling feelings of sure-footedness and confidence. It is so easy to be sarcastic, critical, or cutting, especially when we are feeling down. Don't let yourself (and your children) fall into that "putdown" pattern.

• **Make Your Home a Special Place.** Make it a place that is warm, secure, and safe, a place where the children really belong. Make it a place where you would want to live if you were a growing child. You most certainly don't have to be your child's personal playmate, nor do you have to sacrifice your work on the job or at home to be their constant companion. Even if you are together for just a few hours each day, make those hours special. Turn routine tasks into moments of sharing. Even normally dull jobs like sorting laundry, washing dishes, or scrubbing the floors can be shared. Encourage your child to be with you. Talk together, laugh together while you do what has to be done. Sharing moments means you know each other just a little better each time. And sharing moments tells our children that, above all possible material possessions, they are worth our time, our attention, and our love.

# CHAPTER 8

# When Schools Can Help

When I was a teacher in the New York City school system, a parent came in for a report card conference. Her son was doing quite well in school, and I was really proud of his progress. I spoke in glowing terms of how well he got along with others, and of how well he was doing in his academic subjects. At the end of the conference, as she was about to leave, Johnny's mother said: "Mr. DiGiulio, I know it seems like a minor point, but when you sent the notice home as to when parents should come in for their conferences, the letter started with 'Dear Mr. and Mrs. _____.' My husband and I are divorced. I'd just like to let you know." After she left, I stared at a copy of the notice. "Dear Mr. and Mrs. _____" it read.

The next morning, I went to the office and asked the school secretary if, from then on, we could change the headings on the notices we sent home. "Instead of starting all our letters 'Dear Mr. and Mrs. _____,' can't we just say 'Dear Parent' or maybe 'Dear Blank' and let us teachers fill in the rest?" Her answer, in joking terms, was: "Don't you have more important things to worry about than the headings on the letters, Bob. Do you really think parents care?" I told her that I was a bit embarrassed the previous evening, and I realized that some of my children lived in single parent homes; their parents were separated, divorced, or widowed. "So what?" the principal said as he came by. "Well, I think it's important for us to not make children feel abnormal if there's not a Mr. *and* Mrs. at home." His answer: "Bring it up at the next staff conference."

I did, and I asked the teachers to agree to the slight additional work of writing in the name of the parent or parents. As I spoke, I realized that some of the teachers were single parents, and I could see their support. Within the next week, all the notices from one of the largest public schools in New York City simply began with "Dear _____," and the teachers filled in the appropriate name or names.

A minor point? Maybe. But the whole reason for this short anecdote is this: I have found teachers to be helpful, often greatly sympathetic people, especially where single parents and their children are involved. All you have to do is speak up. That one comment made by Johnny's mother had a small but important effect on the way our school personnel looked at single parent, foster parent, and two-parent homes.

But the relationship between the single parent and the school is not always positive. In a recent survey done by Ann Parks of Parents Without Partners, Incorporated, single parents surveyed said that their most common problem as single parents was "difficulties in schools." In a New York Times article, January 1979, Susan Saiter reported, "Almost half the nation's children will spend at least part of their early years in one-parent homes, according to the Bureau of the Census." Despite this fact, schools are still designed to meet the needs of two-parent homes. For example, it is a problem for the working single parent to visit the school during the day; single parents sometimes face difficulties when trying to register their children in new schools; noncustodial parents are often prohibited from seeing their child's report cards.

## Dealing with Schools as Single Parents

There is little question that insensitivity by school personnel to the role of the single parent can cause needless misery, anguish, and embarrassment to both parent and child. But you will never be able to help change some of these situations, or help your child's teacher to see things in a different light, unless you take the first step. As a single parent, you can head off possible trouble and help the school work for your child, rather than against his or her best interests.

• **First, and Most Important, Tell the Teacher That You Are a Single Parent.** Don't apologize; don't explain unless you feel comfortable in doing so. While it is true that some teachers are not very warm people, most are sincerely interested in children, or they would not be teaching in the first place.

• **Try to Develop an Ongoing, Healthy Relationship with the Teacher.** Take advantage of all notices for PTA meetings and parent-teacher conferences. This will help you know the teacher's viewpoints and, just as important, will let the teacher know yours.

• **Let the Teacher Help.** Although the teacher is a very significant adult influence in your child's life, he or she can never replace or fill in for your former spouse. But the teacher can be a real help to you. For example. You think your child has a problem getting along with other children. Since you are a single parent, you don't have another adult around to "bounce ideas off." The teacher can be an ideal "other adult" to listen to your ideas and respond from not only a professional point of view but a human one as well.

Or if your child seems headed toward some serious behavior problem (such as stealing or lying) and you are wondering what to do, your child's teacher can be a fantastic resource. He or she can suggest how to deal with a suspected problem in ways you might not imagine. In short, use your child's teacher to your child's best advantage. Don't ever give up your responsibility as a parent to the teacher, but don't be afraid to share your thoughts and feelings with him or her. Many teachers are parents, and quite a few are single parents themselves, with problems and feelings very similar to yours.

• **Let the School Know the Custody Arrangements.** If you have custody, register with the school the names of the persons who are permitted to call for and take your child from school during the day and at dismissal.

Don't try to have the school hide your child's records from the noncustodial parent. Unless such a prohibition is specifically spelled out in the custody agreement, you cannot deny the parent's right to know about his or her child's progress in school. According to William B. Riley, special assistant for the Family Educational Rights and Privacy Act in the U.S. Office of Education, there is no federal law prohibiting noncustodial parents from seeing their children's records and following their progress in school. Nor are there state laws to that effect. The only barriers seem to be local school policies. In any event, only a court order can prevent the noncustodial parent from exercising this right (and responsibility).

• **Ask Questions.** Use the teacher's ability and knowledge. Relate to your child's teacher as adult to adult: don't ever be intimidated or put yourself in the position of a child. Find out how well your child works with others, how he or she behaves in different settings and groups. Don't settle for "Harry is doing better in math and is a helpful child. Next parent."

Tell the teacher about some of the things your child does when he or she is not in school. If the teacher seems receptive, go "behind the scenes." You need not pour out your heart, but you do need to share. After all, you are entrusting your child to him or her for at least six hours a day, five days a week.

At times, you might be dissatisfied with the teacher. If, after trying to work out your differences, you feel that there is a real problem or a real personality "clash" between child and teacher, do not be afraid to approach the principal and discuss this matter. If your child has, all of a sudden, started having behavior or learning problems in school, look into it. There is always the possibility that a change of class and teacher might be in order.

• **Confront Stereotypes.** Sometimes—and this must be faced—when a child presents a behavior problem at school, teachers jump to the conclusion that Johnny misbehaves because "his mother is a divorcee," or Mary's difficulties are caused by her "broken home." Such stereotypes are insulting; they do not help you, your child, or the teacher in the search for better, more appropriate behavior. How can you counteract this?

The better you know your child's teacher (and

the better the teacher knows your circumstances) the less likely the teacher will be to jump to conclusions. If you show a willingness to work with the teacher on improving your child's behavior, the chances are slim indeed that he or she will take the easy way out — blaming that which has no bearing on the subject at hand.

If there is a behavior problem, face it squarely yourself. (Don't you blame it on your divorce or widowhood.) Talk over ways to change the misbehavior instead of ways to blame yourself, child, or former spouse.

Do not worry about the reaction of the other children in the school to the fact that yours is a single parent home. There may be some name-calling and cruelty. But, even in the older elementary grades, most children I've seen, urban and rural, have too much sympathy and sense of fair play to annoy a child simply because a parent has died, has separated, or has been through a divorce. Besides, more and more children are living in single parent homes. It's "no big deal" to most children today.

• **Get to Know the Teacher Personally.** Whether you live in a small community, a suburb, or even in a large city, invite the teacher to dinner. This happens quite frequently in my area of Vermont, but it seems to be a "lost custom" in the larger cities. It is not only a caring gesture, but it can help the teacher better know and understand your circumstances. ("Broken home?" Let the teacher see how "broken" your home is. Do your part to help break down some myths about the single-parent home.)

• **Find Time for School.** Many, if not most, teachers and school personnel are willing to meet

81

parents who work full-time at night or even on Saturday mornings.

Even if your job keeps you very busy, or if you're job hunting, take the time to join the PTA or a similar parent organization. The more you know about the school, the greater your influence. Your influence counts. Use it.

If you are planning to move, take just a few hours before making a final decision on where to live, and visit the school your child will attend. Do not take the realtor's word alone on how "excellent" the schools in that district are. Visit the school. Look for alternatives if you wish (private schools, schools affiliated with a religious faith, Montessori schools). The time you take for a look beforehand might save you and your child much anguish later on.

• **Be Assertive with the School.** This is especially necessary when dealing with large schools or hesitant faculty. Keep in mind that the school is there for the children, and not the other way around. You have the right to see all records kept by the school on your child, and, if you wish, you may appeal to the school principal concerning any records that you feel are either useless or derogatory to your child. As a school principal, I regularly go through each child's records to not only know my children better, but also to keep an eye out for "pertinent matter" that serves no useful purpose.

• **Encourage Involvement in School Activities.** School is at times a larger influence on a child's life than even a parent. Recognizing this, you can encourage your child to take part in healthy, stimulating activities offered by the school. Sports, drama, yearbook, band, glee club are all valuable school activities, provided your child's involvement is kept in a balance with other demands and commitments of both you and your child.

• **Meet Other Single Parents.** Some of the larger elementary schools and many high schools organize workshops and discussion groups for their single parents. Find out about them. You might be amazed to learn how similar the problems are that confront other single parents. If there is no such group and if you have the time, consider starting one. This is just one way of giving yourself not only an additional social outlet, but also one that is potentially beneficial to your child as well.

Your role in the education of your child is critical. Go to the school. Get to know the teacher, and let the teacher know about you. Let the teacher know that a special love between parent and child is fully alive and well. Showing that love through interest and caring makes it special. You are asking for help and cooperation from the school; you are not giving up your love and responsibility as a parent. You are a parent and you care deeply for your child. Show it—to the school, the teacher, to yourself, and, always, to your child.

# CHAPTER 9
# Your Personal Life

Just as many single parents feel unsure at times of their authority as parents, they often feel uneasy about their personal lives as well. And, ironically, the people closest to them—children and relatives—can at times provide the greatest barriers to a single parent's desire to seek emotional fulfillment. Children may obstruct a single mother's attempts at dating men, or relatives may bring social pressure to bear when they feel such dating is "wrong." Both children and relatives may even use that most powerful tool—guilt—to control a parent's behavior.

It helps that attitudes today are more relaxed toward dating, remarriage, and parental freedom. But if a child feels threatened, left out, or unfulfilled, he or she is likely to try to prevent the parent's needs from being met. Possessiveness is a normal human feeling and causes no trouble until it gets out of control. The special relationship you have with your child, like all human loving experiences, can be damaged due to possessiveness, jealousy, or a desire to be in charge. By taking just a few precautions, you can protect your relationship with your child and head off attempts to obstruct your personal life now and your possible remarriage in the future.

Examine your relationship with your children. Ask yourself: "Who's in control?" Is it you? Is your child getting his or her way most of the time?

If you are in control, fine. But, what kind of control? If it's a "do as I say and keep still" kind, you are going to have problems later on (if you're not already having them). If your child feels left out, squelched, or thwarted in feeling like a wanted, loved person, he or she will stand in the way of your happiness, as if to say, "Hey, I count, too!" Try for that happy medium, whereby your child feels that his or her needs are being met, while, at the same time, you are the adult-in-charge, and your freedom is not hampered.

If your child is in control, it is almost certain that there will be big problems when you seek the love and companionship of another adult. And it will only get worse as your child grows older. If this is the case, read (or re-read) Chapter Seven for practical assistance in establishing your authority.

In seeking a personal life for yourself, start early. As long as you still consider the time with your child special, don't feel guilty about hiring a baby-sitter. If you feel "left out of life" and lonely for adult company, the odds are great that when you are with your child you won't be a cheery, fun-to-be-with person. By meeting your own needs you will be meeting the needs of your child.

If your life with your children is harmonious, let no one prevent you from seeking personal fulfillment. And that means mother, father, grandparents, former spouse, sister, brother, or "friend" who simply "wants to help." You've been through a lot, and you can't afford to listen when other adults seek to control your life. Relatives can be tremendously helpful, or they can be devastating. Ask yourself when you're getting advice or help: "Is what they're saying going to help me meet my needs? My child's needs?"

Don't feel guilty in meeting your own needs. Guilty feelings do no good. If you want to date or re-marry, that's fine. If you don't, that's fine too. But let no guilt feelings or feelings of self-punishment stand in your way. You need pay for no crime; you've committed none. Although you have a deep, life-long responsibility to be a parent to your children, you do not—ever—need to answer to others for your actions, especially when those actions are your attempts to add adult love to your world.

In *Paradoxes of Everyday Life,* Milton R. Sapirstein said: "It is impossible for any woman to love her children twenty-four hours a day." We can't be perfect mothers, or fathers. We love our children deeply; we love them eternally. But twenty-four hours a day? Impossible. Save a few of those hours, instead, for yourself.

# CHAPTER 10
# You're Not Alone

When you are a parent, you need all the help you can get. When you're a single parent, that help can be even more precious to you. Single parents have many sources of support today, consisting of large and small organizations, groups, and individual help.

In terms of large organizations, there is no more-successful and broad-based group than Parents Without Partners, Inc. At present, PWP has over 165,000 members in the United States and Canada, and there are over one thousand chapters located in large cities and small communities throughout both countries. The only requirement for membership in PWP is that you be a single parent, regardless of custody arrangements. Membership is open to never-married, divorced, adoptive, or widowed single parents. PWP provides support for single parents in various ways, such as providing self-help information, offering understanding and encouragement, holding social activities, arranging discussion groups, or inviting professional speakers for single parent seminars and workshops. In addition, PWP publishes an excellent journal, *The Single Parent*, which is full of practical help and shared experiences of other single parents. Available to members and nonmembers, it is an inexpensive, worthwhile magazine.

For information about joining PWP, subscribing to *The Single Parent*, or starting your own PWP chapter (you'll need a minimum of twenty-five people) write:

Parents Without Partners, Inc.
7910 Woodmont Avenue
Washington, D.C. 20014

In addition to Parents Without Partners, workshops for single parents are often held at local colleges, high schools, adult education centers, and elementary schools. They may consist of discussion groups where single parents can get together and realize that their problems are far from unique, or they may be run like college courses with a classroom-lecture format. Either way, if you can share some ideas, thoughts, and strategies with other single parents, you'll gain valuable assistance in meeting your own needs and situation. Consider starting a single parents group, if there's none nearby.

If you are seeing a counselor, he or she can probably suggest a local group or course to you. Investigate the possibility that your church has a single parents organization. Check newspapers, too, for advertised meetings held at, for example, a YMCA or YWCA. If your children attend a large school, try to find out if there are enough single parents in the PTA who might be interested in starting a discussion group. The support you can gain from other single parents can clarify and reinforce your feelings of competency as a single parent.

If you feel that you are having an especially difficult time coping with being a single parent, don't hesitate to speak to a professional counselor. Even if you're short on cash, there are countless organizations for men, for women, or for both, that are ready to provide counseling or psychological help. Don't be a martyr; it does not help you or your child if you try to suffer in silence.

Even if you are not inclined to speak with a counselor, don't overlook the other people who want to help: your minister, your parish priest, clergyman or clergywoman all have experience with human problems and are some of the best therapists around. Regardless of with whom you choose to speak, don't keep silent; don't try to keep it to yourself as "my problem," because if it is, it is also your child's problem.

Lastly, don't forget friends. Some will drift off if they are married and you're a single parent. And we lose touch with many as we get older. But if you are one of the fortunate ones with at least one good, close friend, use him or her for support. As so well said by W. Somerset Maugham in *The Circle*, friendship is a life-long proposition: "When married people don't get on they can separate, but if they're not married it's impossible. It's a tie that only death can sever."

Focus on your children, because they need you and want to love you; focus on your friends because they're there when you need them, and focus on yourself because you are important, loved, and needed especially when you're a single parent. When you're a single parent, you are not alone.

# Suggestions for Further Reading

Atkin, Edith and Rubin, Estelle. *Part Time Father.* New York: The Vanguard Press, Inc., 1976.
Speaks of the father-child relationship, including the full-time single father.

Cassidy, Robert. *What Every Man Should Know about Divorce.* Washington, D.C.: New Republic Books, 1977.
Probably the most complete sourcebook of information available for divorced men.

Dodson, Fitzhugh. *How to Discipline—with Love.* New York: Rawson Associates, Inc., 1977.
Includes a chapter for the single parent. Well written in a conversational tone; one of the best "discipline" books.

Galper, Miriam. *Co-Parenting: Sharing Your Child Equally.* Philadelphia: Running Press, 1978.
Presents an interesting and practical approach to joint custody, told largely in the first person.

Jackson, Edgar N. *Telling a Child about Death.* New York: Channel Press, 1965.

A sensitive, thoughtful, and practical book for widowed parents.

Klein, Carole. *The Single Parent Experience.* New York: Avon Books, 1973.

One of the first really fine books on the subject of single parenthood.

Losoncy, Larry. *When Your Child Needs a Hug.* St. Meinrad: Abbey Press, 1978.

A warm guide to the importance of nurturing emotional growth in infants, children, and adolescents.

Napolitane, Catherine and Pellegrino, Victoria. *Living and Loving after Divorce.* New York: Rawson Associates, Inc., 1977.

Written for the divorced woman; describes eight stages that follow a divorce. Comprehensive and helpful information written with an open mind.

Thompson, Andrew D. *When Your Child Learns to Choose.* St. Meinrad: Abbey Press, 1978.

Gets right to the point of being a parent: how to help children develop values needed for a lifetime.